PAUL CARDALL

40 HYMNS
FOR FORTY DAYS

Due to licensing restrictions, "Great Is Thy Faithfulness" and
"Upon the Cross of Calvary" are not included in this book.

ISBN 978-1-5400-8345-6

HAL•LEONARD®

Visit Hal Leonard Online at
www.halleonard.com
www.paulcardall.com

Contact us:
Hal Leonard
7777 West Bluemound Road
Milwaukee, WI 53213
Email: info@halleonard.com

In Europe, contact:
Hal Leonard Europe Limited
42 Wigmore Street
Marylebone, London, W1U 2RN
Email: info@halleonardeurope.com

In Australia, contact:
Hal Leonard Australia Pty. Ltd.
4 Lentara Court
Cheltenham, Victoria, 3192 Australia
Email: info@halleonard.com.au

ALL CREATURES OF OUR GOD AND KING

Words by FRANCIS OF ASSISI
Translated by WILLIAM HENRY DRAPER
Music from *Geistliche Kirchengesang*
Arranged by Paul Cardall

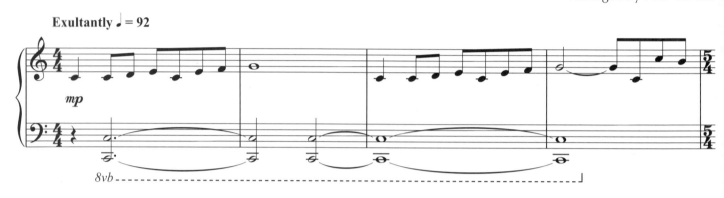

AMAZING GRACE

For piano, cello & violin

Words by JOHN NEWTON
Traditional American Melody
Arranged by Paul Cardall

A reproducible cello/violin part is included on page 110.

COME, FOLLOW ME

Words by JOHN NICHOLSON
Music by SAMUEL McBURNEY
Arranged by Paul Cardall

COME, YE CHILDREN OF THE LORD

Words by JAMES H. WALLIS
Spanish Melody Arranged by BENJAMIN CARR
Arranged by Paul Cardall

13

COUNT YOUR BLESSINGS

Words by JOHNSON OATMAN, JR.
Music by EDWIN O. EXCELL
Arranged by Paul Cardall

DAY OF REST

By PAUL CARDALL

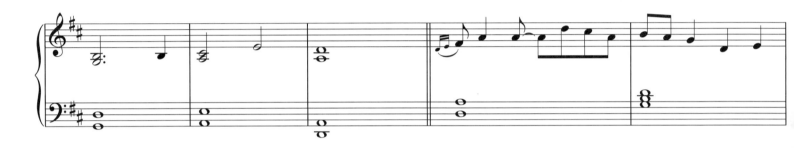

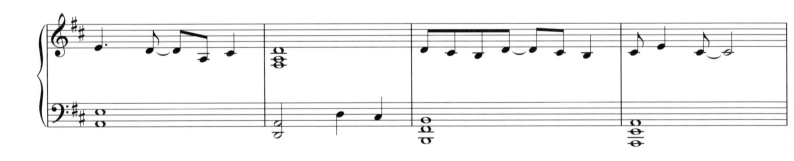

BE STILL, MY SOUL

Words by KATHARINA VON SCHLEGEL
Music by JEAN SIBELIUS
Arranged by Paul Cardall

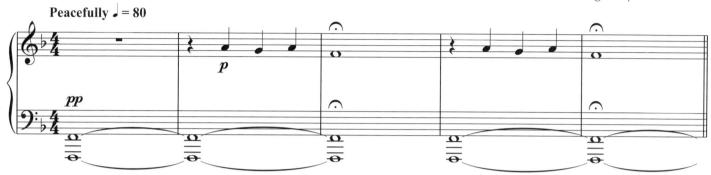

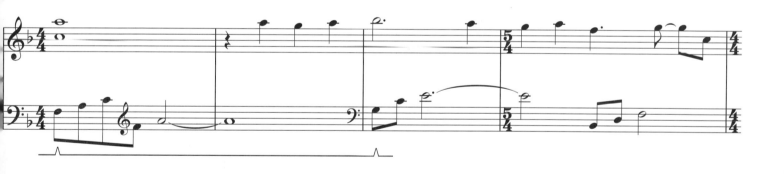

DEAREST CHILDREN, GOD IS NEAR YOU

Words by CHARLES L. WALKER
Music by JOHN MENZIES MacFARLANE
Arranged by Paul Cardall

FATHER IN HEAVEN, WE DO BELIEVE

Words by PARLEY P. PRATT
Music by JANE ROMNEY CRAWFORD
Arranged by Paul Cardall

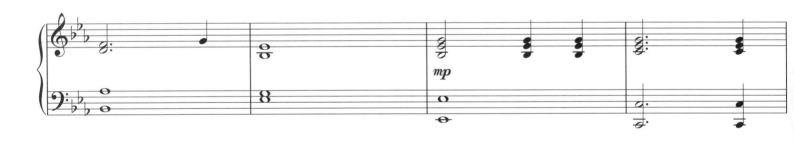

FISHERS OF MEN

By PAUL CARDALL

DID YOU THINK TO PRAY?

Words by MARY A. PEPPER KIDDER
Music by WILLIAM O. PERKINS
Arranged by Paul Cardall

FOR THE BEAUTY OF THE EARTH

Words by FOLLIOT S. PIERPOINT
Music by CONRAD KOCHER
Arranged by Paul Cardall

GENTLY RAISE THE SACRED STRAIN

Words by WILLIAM W. PHELPS
Music by THOMAS C. GRIGGS
Arranged by Paul Cardall

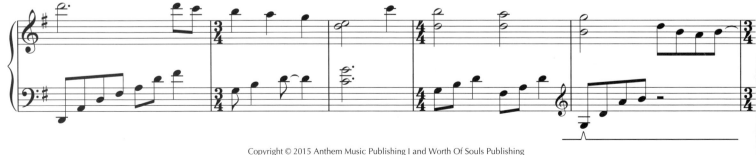

GLORY TO GOD ON HIGH

Words by JAMES ALLEN
Music by FELICE DE GIARDINI
Arranged by Paul Cardall

With dignity ♩ = 76

GOD IS LOVE

Words by THOMAS R. TAYLOR
Music by THOMAS C. GRIGGS
Arranged by Paul Cardall

Gently ♩ = 80

GOD, OUR FATHER, HEAR US PRAY

Words by ANNIE PINNOCK MALIN
Music by LOUIS M. GOTTSCHALK
Arranged by Paul Cardall

Worshipfully ♩ = 80

HIGH ON THE MOUNTAIN TOP

Words by JOEL H. JOHNSON
Music by EBENEZER BEESLEY
Arranged by Paul Cardall

HOW FIRM A FOUNDATION

Words attributed to ROBERT KEEN
Music attributed to J. ELLIS
Arranged by Paul Cardall

I NEED THEE EVERY HOUR

Words by ANNIE S. HAWKS
Music by ROBERT LOWRY
Arranged by Paul Cardall

Rubato

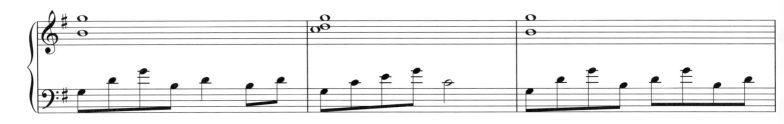

I'LL GO WHERE YOU WANT ME TO GO

Words by MARY BROWN and CHARLES E. PRIOR
Music by CARRIE E. ROUNSEFELL
Arranged by Paul Cardall

IN THE GARDEN

Words and Music by
C. AUSTIN MILES
Arranged by Paul Cardall

ISRAEL, ISRAEL, GOD IS CALLING

Words by RICHARD SMYTH
Music by CHARLES C. CONVERSE
Arranged by Paul Cardall

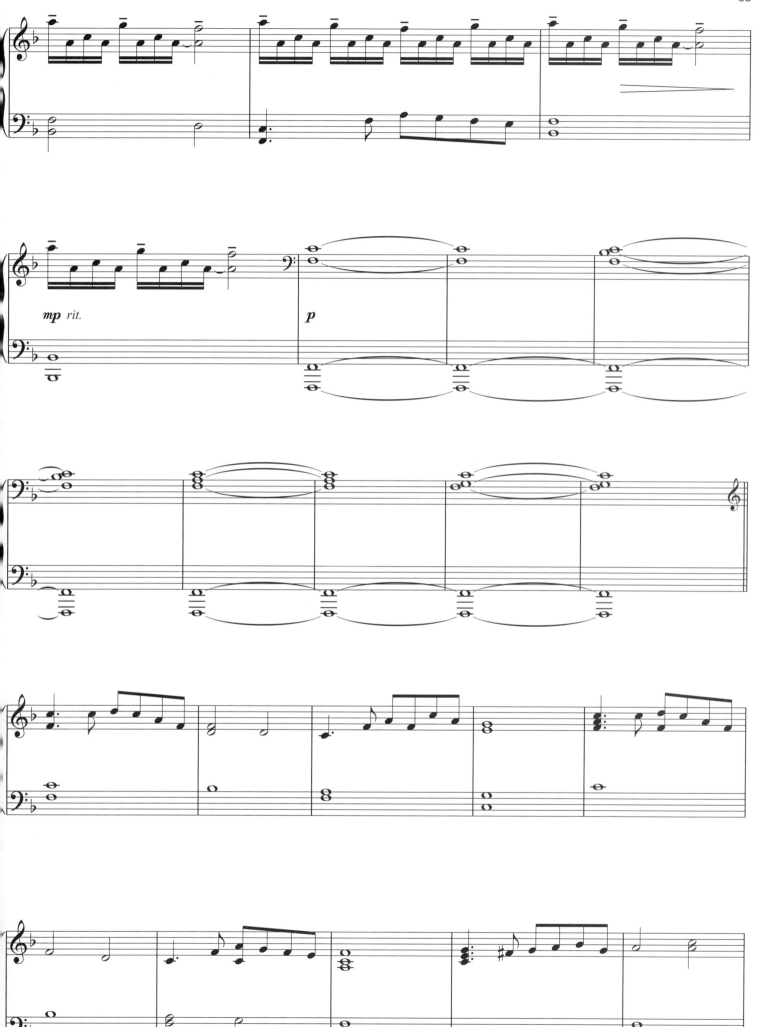

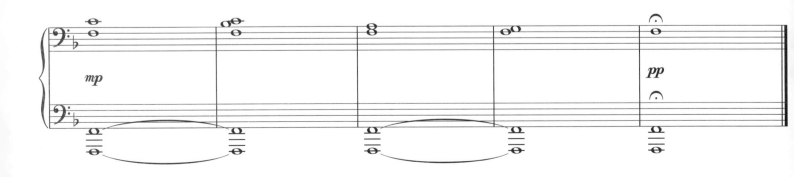

GOD BE WITH YOU
TILL WE MEET AGAIN

Words by JEREMIAH E. RANKIN
Music by WILLIAM G. TOMER
Arranged by Paul Cardall

JESUS SAID LOVE EVERYONE

Words and Music by
MOISELLE RENSTROM
Arranged by Paul Cardall

JESUS, THE VERY THOUGHT OF THEE

Words attributed to BERNARD OF CLAIRVAUX
Music by JOHN BACCHUS DYKES
Arranged by Paul Cardall

Slow rubato throughout

JESUS WANTS ME FOR A SUNBEAM

Words by NELLIE TALBOT
Music by EDWIN O. EXCELL
Arranged by Paul Cardall

8vb

LEAD, KINDLY LIGHT

Words by JOHN HENRY NEWMAN
Music by JOHN B. DYKES
Arranged by Paul Cardall

Rubato throughout

THE LORD IS MY SHEPHERD

Words by JAMES MONTGOMERY
Music by THOMAS KOSCHAT
Arranged by Paul Cardall

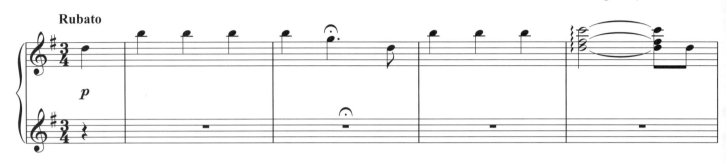

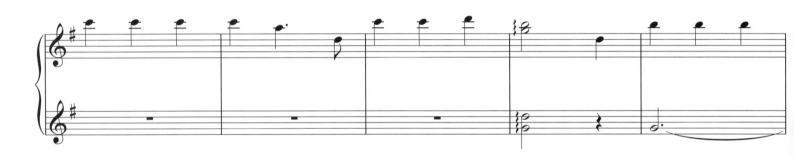

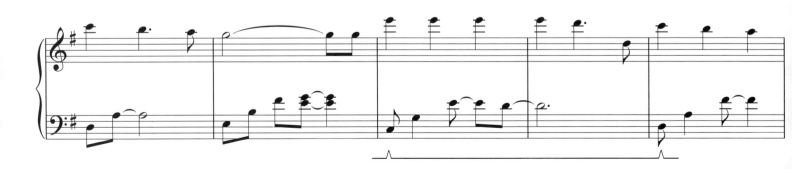

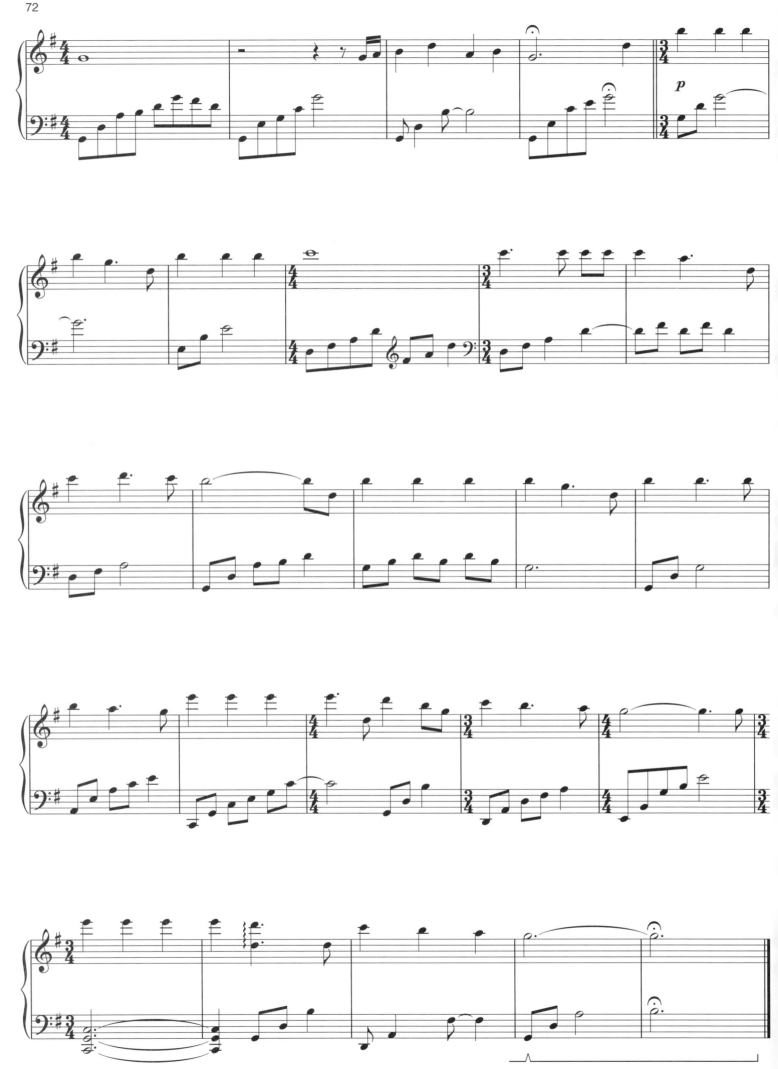

LORD, WE ASK THEE ERE WE PART

Words by GEORGE MANWARING
Music by BENJAMIN MILGROVE
Arranged by Paul Cardall

THE MORNING BREAKS

Words by PARLEY P. PRATT
Music by GEORGE CARELESS
Arranged by Paul Cardall

With reverent conviction ♩ = 100

NOW LET US REJOICE

Words by WILLIAM W. PHELPS
Music by HENRY TUCKER
Arranged by Paul Cardall

A POOR WAYFARING MAN OF GRIEF

Words by JAMES MONTGOMERY
Music by GEORGE COLES
Arranged by Paul Cardall

REDEEMER OF ISRAEL

Words by WILLIAM W. PHELPS and JOSEPH SWAIN
Music by FREEMAN LEWIS
Arranged by Paul Cardall

THE SPIRIT OF GOD

Words by WILLIAM W. PHELPS
Traditional Melody
Arranged by Paul Cardall

SWEET HOUR OF PRAYER

Words by WILLIAM W. WALFORD
Music by WILLIAM B. BRADBURY
Arranged by Paul Cardall

With feeling ♩ = 72

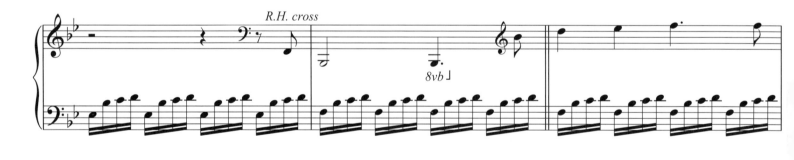

THERE IS A GREEN HILL FAR AWAY

Words by CECIL FRANCES ALEXANDER
Music by JOHN H. GOWER
Arranged by Paul Cardall

TRUTH REFLECTS UPON OUR SENSES

Words by ELIZA R. SNOW and M.E. ABBEY
Music by CHARLES DAVIS TILLMAN
Arranged by Paul Cardall

Thoughtfully ♩ = 80

WE THANK THEE, O GOD, FOR A PROPHET

Words by WILLIAM FOWLER
Music by CAROLINE SHERIDAN NORTON
Arranged by Paul Cardall

THERE IS SUNSHINE IN MY SOUL TODAY

Words by ELIZABETH E. HEWITT
Music by JOHN R. SWENEY
Arranged by Paul Cardall

WERE YOU THERE?

Traditional Spiritual
Arranged by Paul Cardall

AMAZING GRACE

Cello
Violin

Words by JOHN NEWTON
Traditional American Melody
Arranged by Paul Cardall

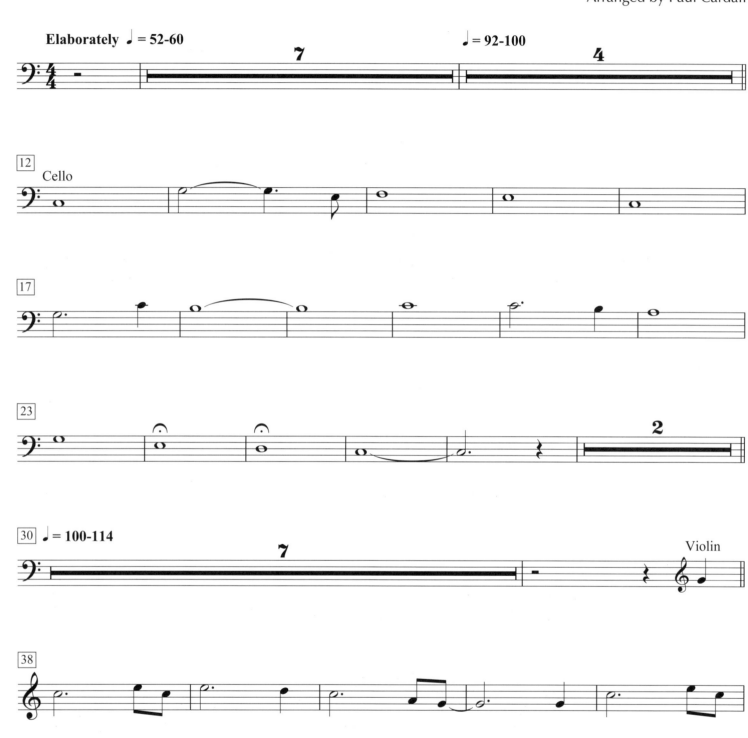

Permission is granted by the publisher to copy this score for performance purposes only.

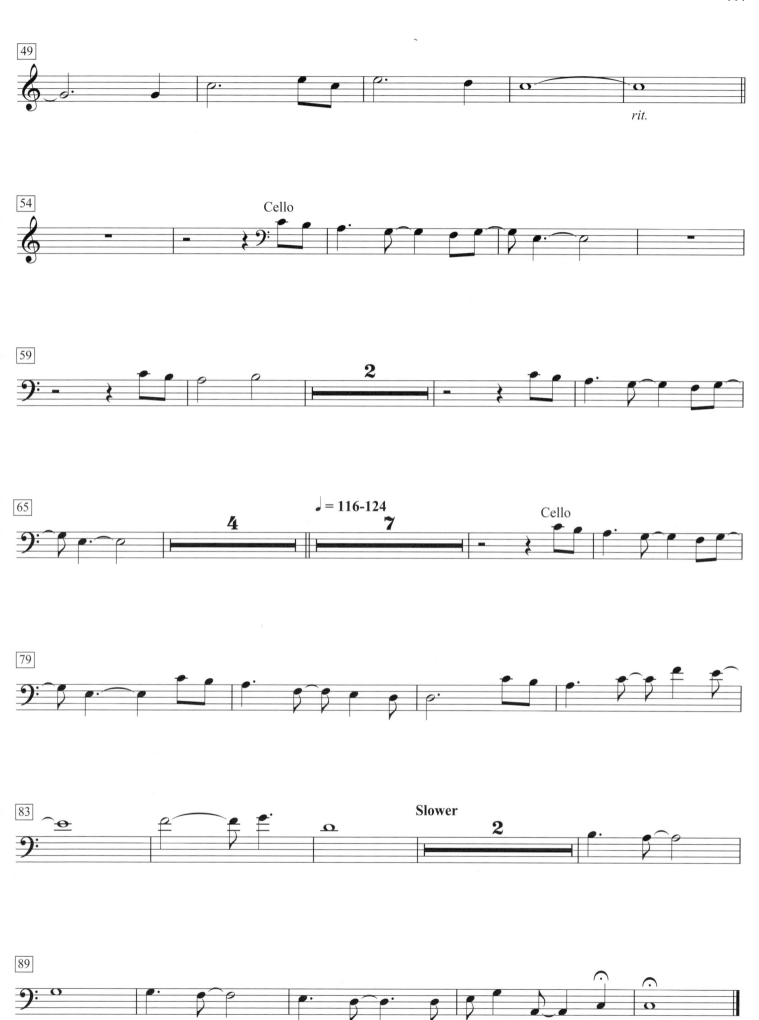